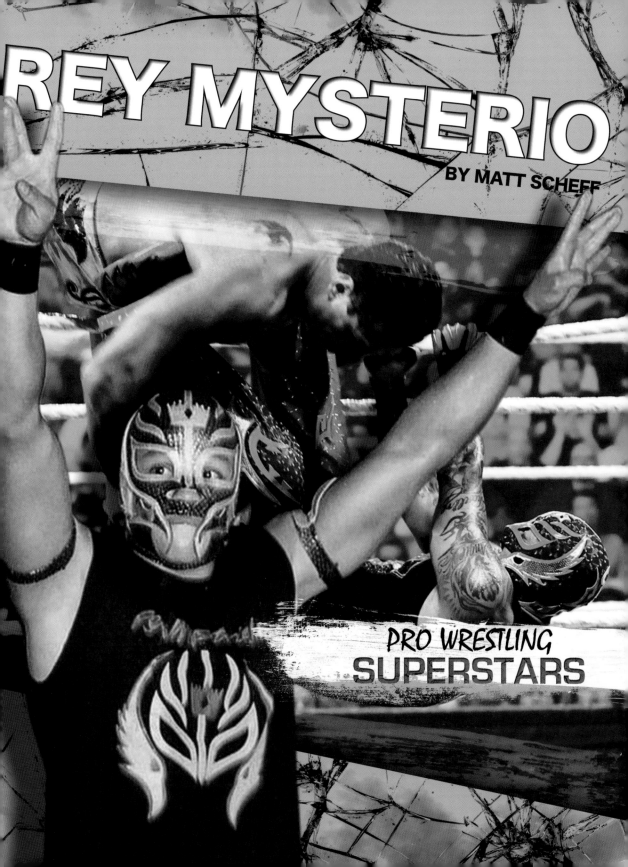

REY MYSTERIO

BY MATT SCHEFF

PRO WRESTLING
SUPERSTARS

Published by ABDO Publishing Company, PO Box 398166, Minneapolis, MN 55439. Copyright © 2014 by Abdo Consulting Group, Inc. International copyrights reserved in all countries. No part of this book may be reproduced in any form without written permission from the publisher. SportsZone™ is a trademark and logo of ABDO Publishing Company.

Printed in the United States of America,
North Mankato, Minnesota
082013
012014

Editor: Chrös McDougall
Series Designer: Jake Nordby

Photo Credits: Mike Lano Photojournalism, cover, 1, 10-11; St. Louis Post-Dispatch, J.B. Forbes/AP Images, cover (background), 1 (background), 28-29; Matt Roberts/ZUMA Press/Icon SMI, 4-5, 20-21, 23, 26-27, 30 (bottom); Rick Scuteri/AP Images, 7 (inset), 22, 30 (top); Lenny Ignelzi/AP Images, 6-7; Scott Heppell/AP Images, 8-9; Tammie Arroyo/AP Images, 12; Elsa/Getty Images, 13; Rajesh Nirgude/AP Images, 14-15; Daniel Kramer/ABACAUSA.COM/Newscom, 16-17; Paul Abell/AP Images for WWE, 18-19, 31; La Nacion de Costa Rica/Newscom, 24-25

Library of Congress Control Number: 2013945692

Cataloging-in-Publication Data

Scheff, Matt.
  Rey Mysterio / Matt Scheff.
    p. cm. -- (Pro wrestling superstars)
Includes index.
ISBN 978-1-62403-137-3
1. Rey Mysterio--Juvenile literature. 2. Wrestlers--United States--Biography--Juvenile literature. 1. Title.
796.812092--dc23
[B]

2013945692

CONTENTS

Rey Mysterio Jr. electrifies wrestling fans with his high-flying moves.

WRESTLEMANIA 22

The crowd at WrestleMania 22 roared as three men entered the ring. It was a Triple Threat match. Kurt Angle, Randy Orton, and Rey Mysterio would battle it out for the World Wrestling Entertainment (WWE) heavyweight championship.

After a long battle, Mysterio threw Angle out of the ring. Then he hit Orton with a West Coast Pop. Mysterio flew off the top rope. He drove Orton to the mat and pinned him. Mysterio was the new heavyweight champion!

BORN TO WRESTLE

Rey Mysterio's real name is Oscar Gutierrez. He was born December 11, 1974, in San Diego, California. As a kid, Gutierrez loved to watch a form of Mexican professional wrestling called *lucha libre*. His uncle was a famous wrestler in Mexico and went by the name Rey Misterio. Gutierrez dreamed of joining him in the ring.

Mysterio flies through the air at WrestleMania 26.

San Diego, California

BECOMING MYSTERIO

Gutierrez began training with his uncle in Mexico at age 13. A year later, he wrestled in his first lucha libre match. He used the name Colibri. Later, he changed his wrestling name to Rey Misterio Jr. Misterio was smaller than most of his opponents. He couldn't overpower them. So he used a high-flying, acrobatic wrestling style instead. Fans loved it.

Mexican lucha libre wrestlers are known for their masks.

Mysterio wrestles in a match in Mexico.

Gutierrez and his uncle often wrestled together in tag-team matches in Mexico. Later, Gutierrez changed the spelling of his name to Mysterio. One of his best friends was Dionicio Castellanos Torres. Torres wrestled as Psicosis. The friends began a feud in the ring. They acted like they hated each other. Fans loved their exciting matches. Mysterio's fame grew.

Psicosis, right, was Rey Mysterio's rival.

COMING TO THE UNITED STATES

In 1995, Mysterio left Mexico to return to the United States. He and Psicosis both signed with Extreme Championship Wrestling (ECW). They continued their feud for American fans. A year later, Mysterio joined World Championship Wrestling (WCW). He fought in WCW's cruiserweight division. It was a division for smaller, lighter wrestlers. They were known for their high-flying skills. Mysterio fit right in. He won his first cruiserweight title in July 1996.

Mysterio and Chris Jericho duke it out during a 1998 match.

Mysterio entertains kids on a visit to India.

Gutierrez married his wife, Angie, in 1996. The couple had two children. Gutierrez has their names, Dominik and Aalyah, tattooed on his arms.

The late 1990s and early 2000s were a tough time for Mysterio. WCW forced him to take off his mask in 1999. The decision made Mysterio sad. He felt he was turning his back on his lucha libre roots. Then in 2001, WCW went out of business. Mysterio returned to Mexico to wrestle.

JOINING WWE

Mysterio soon returned to the United States. He joined WWE and won his first match against Chavo Guerrero. WWE fans loved Mysterio's style. He teamed up with Edge to win a tag-team championship in 2002. A year later, he beat Matt Hardy to claim the WWE cruiserweight title.

Mysterio flies high at WrestleMania 25.

FAST FACT

Wrestlers must weigh less than 215 pounds (97.5 kg) to wrestle as cruiserweights. Mysterio weighs just 175 pounds!

Mysterio executes a 619 on Cody Rhodes.

FAST FACT

Mysterio named his finishing move the 619 after the telephone area code of his hometown, San Diego.

Mysterio needed a big finishing move for WWE, so he created the 619. He places his opponent's head over the second rope. Then he steps back and charges, grabbing the ropes and swinging his legs through the second and third ropes. His feet smash into his opponent's head. This powerful move helped make Mysterio a WWE Superstar.

Mysterio celebrates at WrestleMania in 2009.

THE LIGHTEST HEAVYWEIGHT

Mysterio was ready to take on all of WWE's biggest stars. In 2006, he competed in the Royal Rumble. He was the second of 30 wrestlers to enter the ring. More than an hour later, Mysterio was left in the ring with Randy Orton and Triple H. It looked like Mysterio would be thrown out of the ring twice. Both times he grabbed the top rope, wrapped his legs around the opponent, and threw the opponent out instead. Mysterio had won the Royal Rumble!

Mysterio slams his head into CM Punk.

Later in 2006, Mysterio pinned Orton to become the lightest heavyweight champ in WWE history. He held the title for more than three months. In 2008, Mysterio defeated John "Bradshaw" Layfield in just 21 seconds to win the intercontinental championship. He regained his heavyweight title in 2010 in a Fatal 4-Way match against Big Show, CM Punk, and Jack Swagger. Mysterio hit Swagger with a 619 and then jumped off the top rope into the pin.

FAST FACT

Mysterio performed a rap called "Crossing Borders" for an album titled *WWE Originals*.

In early 2011, WWE set up a tournament to crown a new WWE champ. Mysterio advanced to the final. His opponent, the Miz, was in command late in the match. But Mysterio dodged one of the Miz's big moves. Then he finished him off with a 619 to claim the belt.

Mysterio soars through the air to attack Chris Jericho.

Mysterio battles Cody Rhodes at WrestleMania in 2011.

UNCLEAR FUTURE

Mysterio suffered a terrible knee injury in August 2011. He was out of wrestling for almost a year. He returned in July 2012. But he wasn't the same. Mysterio had several title shots. But he couldn't win a belt. And injuries continued to be a problem. In 2013, Mysterio hurt his knee again during an attack by Mark Henry. Some wonder whether he will ever be able to come back.

Rey Mysterio's greatest wrestling days might be behind him. But he still has much to offer. Mysterio has been a mentor to up-and-coming star Sin Cara. Like Mysterio, Sin Cara started out as a lucha libre wrestler. With Mysterio's help, Sin Cara might one day dominate WWE just as his mentor did.

Fast Fact

Mysterio wrote an autobiography in 2009. It's called *Rey Mysterio: Behind the Mask*.

Mysterio flips Alberto Del Rio over the top rope.

TIMELINE

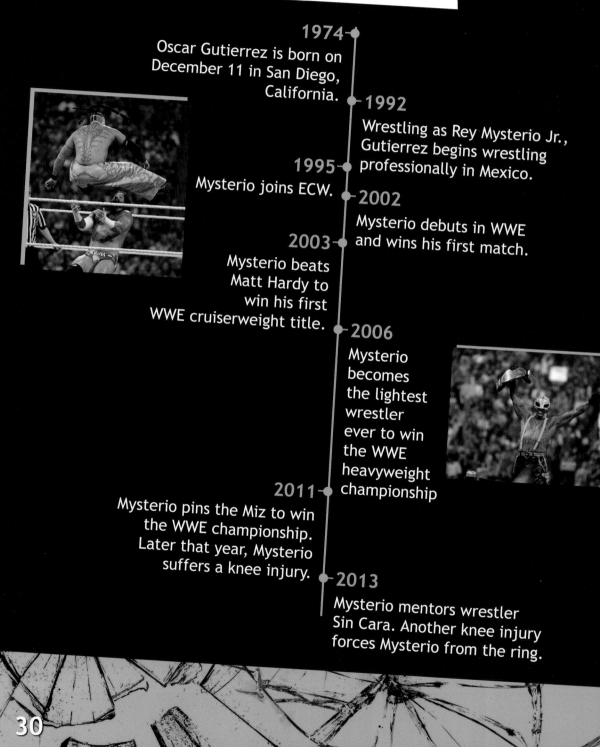

1974
Oscar Gutierrez is born on December 11 in San Diego, California.

1992
Wrestling as Rey Mysterio Jr., Gutierrez begins wrestling professionally in Mexico.

1995
Mysterio joins ECW.

2002
Mysterio debuts in WWE and wins his first match.

2003
Mysterio beats Matt Hardy to win his first WWE cruiserweight title.

2006
Mysterio becomes the lightest wrestler ever to win the WWE heavyweight championship

2011
Mysterio pins the Miz to win the WWE championship. Later that year, Mysterio suffers a knee injury.

2013
Mysterio mentors wrestler Sin Cara. Another knee injury forces Mysterio from the ring.

GLOSSARY

619
Rey Mysterio's finishing move, which features a swinging kick to the head of an opponent draped over the second rope.

autobiography
A book about one's own life.

cruiserweight
A wrestler who weighs 215 pounds (97.5 kg) or less.

Fatal 4-Way match
A wrestling match with traditional rules but four participants.

feud
An intense, long-lasting conflict between wrestlers.

finishing move
A powerful move that a wrestler uses to finish off an opponent.

lucha libre
A style of Mexican wrestling that is famous for its masked wrestlers and acrobatic moves.

mentor
Somebody with much experience who teaches his trade to someone younger or less experienced.

Triple Threat match
A match in which three wrestlers battle at the same time. The first wrestler to pin either of his opponents wins the match.

West Coast Pop
A move in which a wrestler jumps off the top rope, lands on his opponent's shoulders, and drives him to the mat.

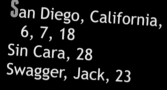